PIRATES

TRUE STORIES OF SEAFARING ROGUES

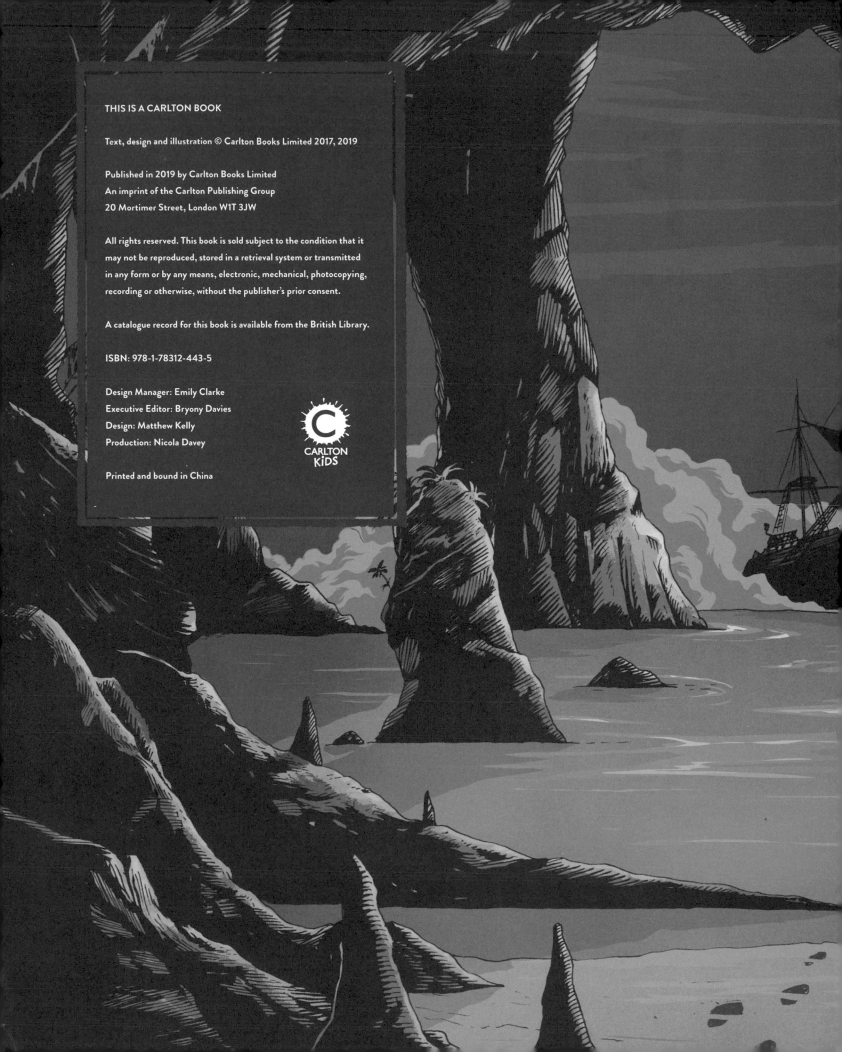

PIRATES

TRUE STORIES OF SEAFARING ROGUES

WRITTEN BY ANNE ROONEY
ILLUSTRATED BY JOE WILSON

WHO WOULD WANT TO BE A PIRATE? 6

LORDS OF LAND AND SEA 8

MEDITERRANEAN MARAUDERS 10

HUNTING GROUNDS OF THE CORSAIRS 12

THE BARBAROSSA BROTHERS 14

HOW TO BE A BARBARY CORSAIR 16

THE LOATHSOME LIFE OF A GALLEY SLAVE 18

A SEA HELD TO RANSOM 20

PIRATE GOLD 22

PIRATES OF THE CARIBBEAN 24

THE HUNT FOR TREASURE 26

BLACKBEARD 28

LIVE LIKE A PIRATE 30

THE PIRATE'S CODE 32

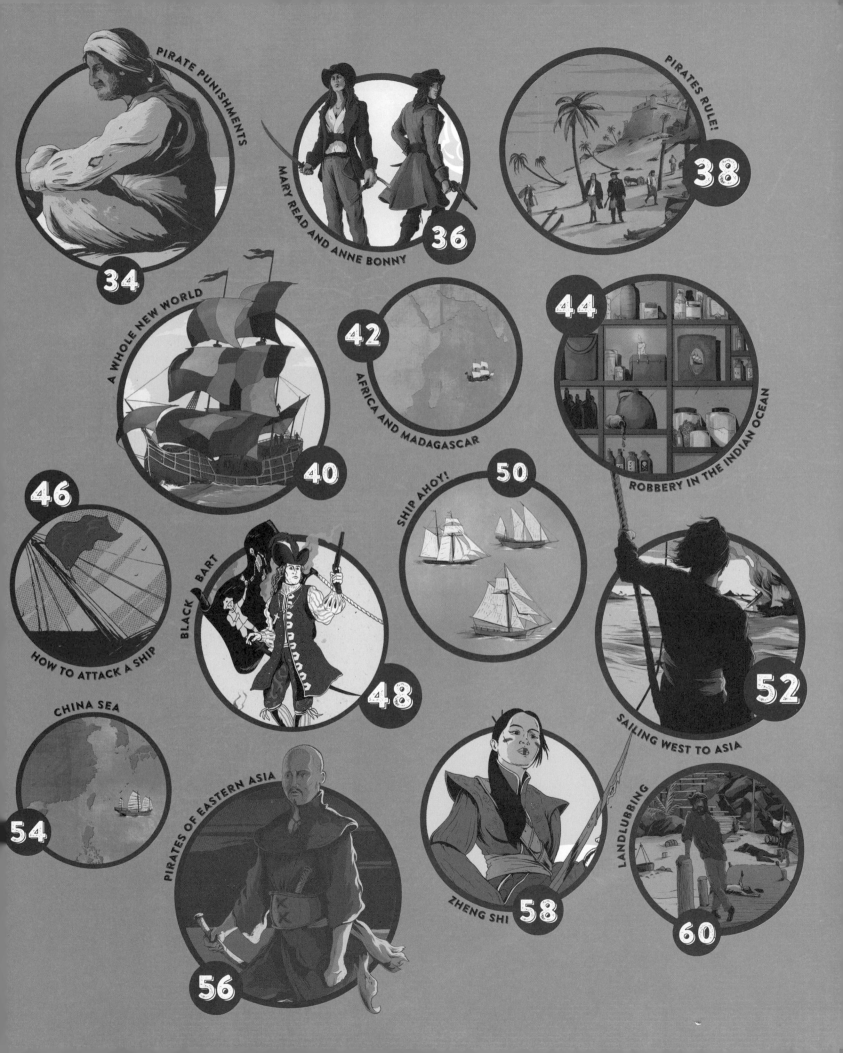

PIRATE PUNISHMENTS **34**

MARY READ AND ANNE BONNY **36**

PIRATES RULE! **38**

A WHOLE NEW WORLD **40**

AFRICA AND MADAGASCAR **42**

ROBBERY IN THE INDIAN OCEAN **44**

HOW TO ATTACK A SHIP **46**

BLACK BART **48**

SHIP AHOY! **50**

SAILING WEST TO ASIA **52**

CHINA SEA **54**

PIRATES OF EASTERN ASIA **56**

ZHENG SHI **58**

LANDLUBBING **60**

WHO WOULD WANT TO BE A PIRATE?

THE PROMISE OF RICHES, ADVENTURE AND EXOTIC LANDS, WEIGHED AGAINST A TOUGH LIFE AT HOME, HAS ALWAYS MADE PIRATE LIFE ATTRACTIVE. BUT WHAT WAS THE REALITY?

A PIRATE'S LIFE FOR ME?

A pirate could earn more in a single trip than his honest friends could earn in a lifetime. But pirates were and are vicious criminals, known and feared for their cruelty. Life at sea is dangerous. In the past, pirate-hunters, shipwreck, disease and the perils of battle meant that most pirates died young. They paid a high price for the promises of piracy.

WHO WERE THE PIRATES' PREY?

Some pirates, such as the Vikings, raided the land, launching stealthy assaults by night, or all-out violent attacks in broad daylight. Others attacked ships at sea, using fast, nimble boats to hunt trading ships weighed down with cargo. Even small fishing boats and local traders were robbed of food and tools.

In the Golden Age of piracy, the most sought-after targets were Spanish treasure galleons, and merchant ships packed with silks, ivory, jade and jewels. The pirates stole the cargo or the whole ship, killing, kidnapping or marooning the crew.

WERE ALL PIRATES CRIMINALS?

Not all pirates joined up willingly. Some were captured from raided ships or towns and forced to become pirates – or face death or slavery. In some places, fishermen or loggers turned to piracy when work was scarce.

Many pirates started as privateers, who were paid to attack a state's enemies by sea or on land. If a ruler made peace with an enemy, the privateers became out of work. As the only work they knew was robbery, they carried on doing it, but for their own profit – as pirates.

WHO WERE THE FIRST PIRATES?

There have probably been pirates since humans first made boats to travel the waterways of the world. We know that in 694 BC, an Assyrian king tried to rid the sea around Persia (modern-day Iran) of pirates.

Pirates plagued the Ancient Egyptians, Greeks and Romans, too. They terrorized the seas around China and India for thousands of years. Some were part-time pirates, acting in small bands or from a single boat, while others were part of vast pirate fleets.

WHEN WAS THE GOLDEN AGE OF PIRACY?

The pirates we all know about, the swashbuckling heroes of films and stories, were the pirates of the Golden Age. During the 1600s and 1700s, European and North American pirates marauded the Caribbean Sea, the Indian Ocean, the China Sea and the Mediterranean Sea. They searched for gold, flew pirate flags, and had names like Blackbeard and Captain Devil. The legends live on, but the reality was not so glamorous.

PIRATE PORKIES

Pirates had wooden legs, eye patches, parrots and treasure maps, and made their enemies walk the plank. Right? Wrong, mostly.

Pirates rarely survived serious injury and a disabled pirate would have had a hard time. A pirate who lost an eye or leg usually died or retired. Pirates rarely buried the treasure they stole, and they didn't make people walk the plank – it was far easier to throw them overboard. Punishments for pirates who broke the pirate code were worse still. Some pirates may have taken parrots from South America or Africa to sell – they were valuable. But a pet parrot wouldn't have survived long on a ship full of hungry pirates.

GOLDEN AGE PIRATES

The Golden Age of piracy from the 1600s to the 1720s saw European and North American pirates raiding the treasure ships and merchant traders sailing to and from newly explored lands around the Caribbean, Atlantic, Indian Ocean, China Sea and even the Pacific.

BARBARY CORSAIRS

Fierce pirates based along the coast of North Africa plagued European shipping and merchant traders in the Mediterranean and even out into the Atlantic from the 1500s until the 1820s.

ATLANTIC OCEAN

CARIBBEAN SEA

LORDS OF
LAND
AND
SEA

MOST SEAS AND COASTLINES HAVE SEEN THEIR FAIR SHARE OF PIRATES. WHERE THERE ARE RICH PICKINGS, THERE ARE PIRATES TO PINCH THEM.

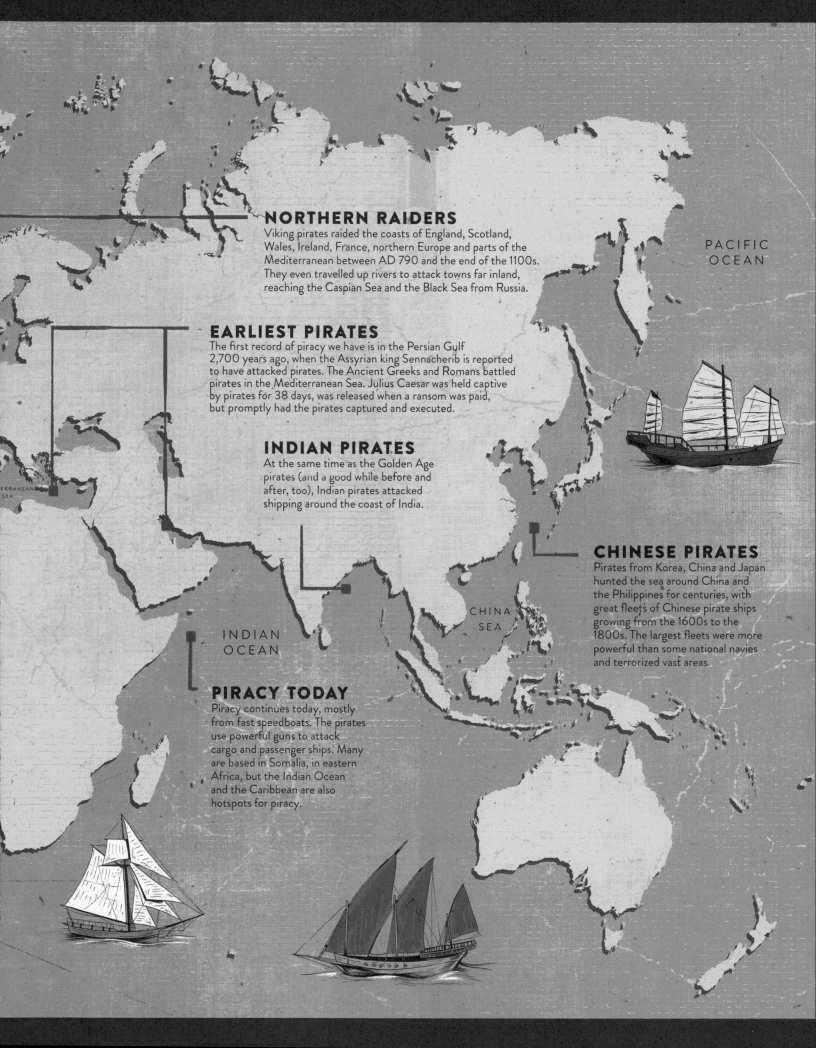

NORTHERN RAIDERS

Viking pirates raided the coasts of England, Scotland, Wales, Ireland, France, northern Europe and parts of the Mediterranean between AD 790 and the end of the 1100s. They even travelled up rivers to attack towns far inland, reaching the Caspian Sea and the Black Sea from Russia.

PACIFIC OCEAN

EARLIEST PIRATES

The first record of piracy we have is in the Persian Gulf 2,700 years ago, when the Assyrian king Sennacherib is reported to have attacked pirates. The Ancient Greeks and Romans battled pirates in the Mediterranean Sea. Julius Caesar was held captive by pirates for 38 days, was released when a ransom was paid, but promptly had the pirates captured and executed.

INDIAN PIRATES

At the same time as the Golden Age pirates (and a good while before and after, too), Indian pirates attacked shipping around the coast of India.

CHINESE PIRATES

Pirates from Korea, China and Japan hunted the sea around China and the Philippines for centuries, with great fleets of Chinese pirate ships growing from the 1600s to the 1800s. The largest fleets were more powerful than some national navies and terrorized vast areas.

MEDITERRANEAN SEA

CHINA SEA

INDIAN OCEAN

PIRACY TODAY

Piracy continues today, mostly from fast speedboats. The pirates use powerful guns to attack cargo and passenger ships. Many are based in Somalia, in eastern Africa, but the Indian Ocean and the Caribbean are also hotspots for piracy.

MEDITERRANEAN MARAUDERS

THE MEDITERRANEAN WAS A DANGEROUS PLACE IN THE 1500S. A TRIP ACROSS THE SEA, OR EVEN A STROLL ALONG THE BEACH, MIGHT END IN CAPTURE BY PIRATES KNOWN AS THE BARBARY CORSAIRS.

LAWFUL PIRATES?

For more than 300 years in Europe, ruthless and fearsome Muslim pirates called corsairs patrolled the sea and raided the land, taking not just gold and treasure but human captives, too.

The Barbary corsairs were privateers — they had official licences to attack ships and raid enemy lands. The licences came from the rulers of the Barbary states along the coast of North Africa, such as Tunisia and Algeria.

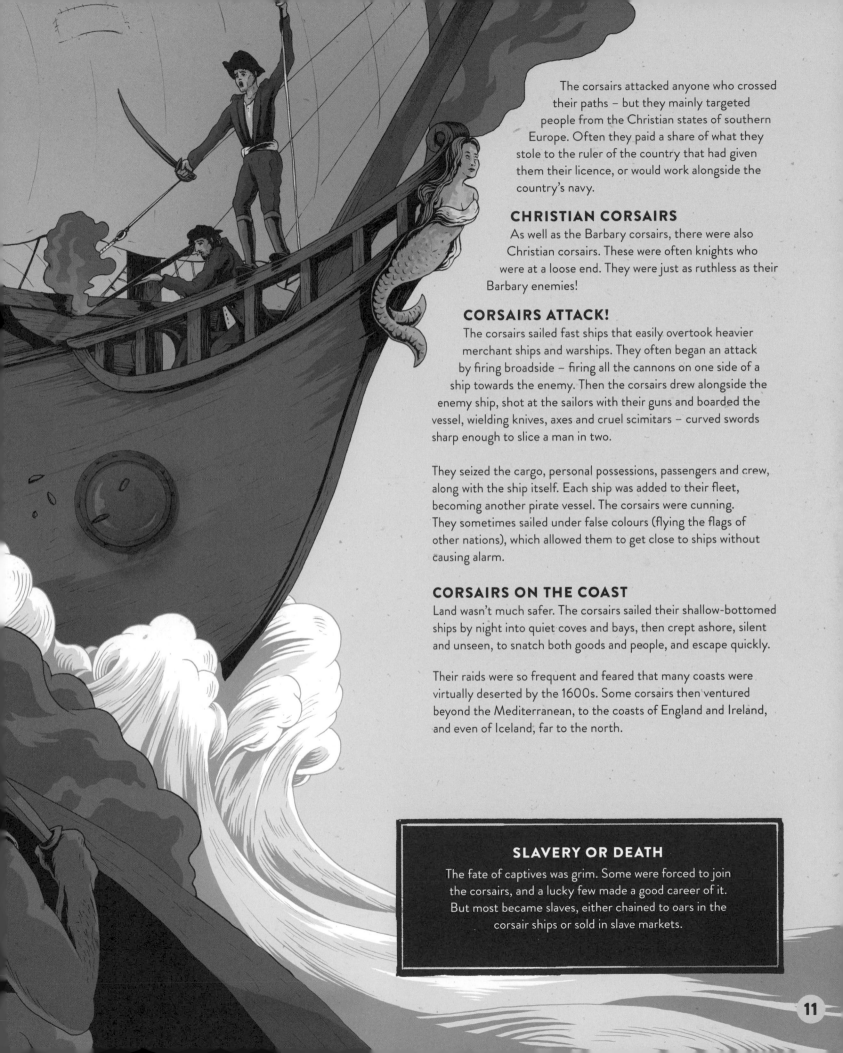

The corsairs attacked anyone who crossed their paths – but they mainly targeted people from the Christian states of southern Europe. Often they paid a share of what they stole to the ruler of the country that had given them their licence, or would work alongside the country's navy.

CHRISTIAN CORSAIRS

As well as the Barbary corsairs, there were also Christian corsairs. These were often knights who were at a loose end. They were just as ruthless as their Barbary enemies!

CORSAIRS ATTACK!

The corsairs sailed fast ships that easily overtook heavier merchant ships and warships. They often began an attack by firing broadside – firing all the cannons on one side of a ship towards the enemy. Then the corsairs drew alongside the enemy ship, shot at the sailors with their guns and boarded the vessel, wielding knives, axes and cruel scimitars – curved swords sharp enough to slice a man in two.

They seized the cargo, personal possessions, passengers and crew, along with the ship itself. Each ship was added to their fleet, becoming another pirate vessel. The corsairs were cunning. They sometimes sailed under false colours (flying the flags of other nations), which allowed them to get close to ships without causing alarm.

CORSAIRS ON THE COAST

Land wasn't much safer. The corsairs sailed their shallow-bottomed ships by night into quiet coves and bays, then crept ashore, silent and unseen, to snatch both goods and people, and escape quickly.

Their raids were so frequent and feared that many coasts were virtually deserted by the 1600s. Some corsairs then ventured beyond the Mediterranean, to the coasts of England and Ireland, and even of Iceland, far to the north.

SLAVERY OR DEATH

The fate of captives was grim. Some were forced to join the corsairs, and a lucky few made a good career of it. But most became slaves, either chained to oars in the corsair ships or sold in slave markets.

IRISH PIRACY

1560s: Grace O'Malley inherited her father's shipping business and soon started acts of piracy. Her fleet held up merchant ships and made them pay to sail on unharmed.

FEARSOME FROM AFAR

1631: Barbary corsairs abducted nearly everyone from the Irish village of Baltimore.

STEALING FISHERMEN

1640, Penzance: Corsairs attacked six boats in one night and forced the fishermen on board into slavery.

TAKEN AT SEA

1609–1616: Barbary corsairs took a total of 466 British vessels.

ATLANTIC OCEAN

DANGEROUS COASTS

Parts of the Spanish, French and Italian coastlines were raided so regularly by corsairs that they were deserted – everyone had fled inland or been kidnapped.

MAP KEY

 GHOST TOWN

 PIRATE ATTACK

 PIRATE BATTLE

 PIRATE HAUNT

A CORSAIR ECONOMY

1580–1620, Algiers: corsairing was the main money-making activity here. Barbary corsairs made travel across the Mediterranean almost impossible.

MEDITERRANEAN SEA

A TIGHT SQUEEZE

Corsairs easily controlled the Straits of Gibraltar – a narrow passage connecting the Mediterranean Sea to the Atlantic Ocean.

AN ARMLESS PIRATE

1512, Bejaïa: here 'Arūj Barbarossa lost an arm fighting against the Spanish.

PIRATE STRONGHOLD

Barbary corsairs' strongholds along the coast of North Africa included Salé, Algiers, Tunis and Tripoli. Here they could safely sell captured slaves and trade their plunder.

SHIP ABLAZE

1803: Stephen Decatur of the US navy recaptured its ship *Philadelphia*, then set it alight in Tunis harbour to prevent privateers seizing it back.

OUTNUMBERED

1518, Tlemcen: 'Arūj Barbarossa was killed by an alliance of Spanish, Holy Roman Empire and African Berber troops after defending his city for 20 days.

HUNTING GROUNDS OF THE CORSAIRS

FOR THREE HUNDRED YEARS, SAVAGE PIRATES PLAGUED THE MEDITERRANEAN AND THE ATLANTIC, ATTACKING SHIPS AND COASTLINE ALIKE.

SNUBBING THE POPE

1504, Elba: the Barbarossa brothers seized two of the Pope's galleys and a ship filled with Spanish knights and soldiers.

LIPARI

1504: the Barbarossa brothers captured the *Cavalleria*, a Sicilian warship with 380 Spanish soldiers and 60 Spanish knights on board.

TERRORIZED ISLAND

Almost the whole island of Corfu was sacked by Khayr al-Dīn Barbarossa in 1537. Many of its people were taken into slavery.

BARBAROSSA BASE

La Goulette, Tunis, was the Barbarossa brothers' lair. From here they ravaged the Mediterranean, paying a share of their plunder to the ruler of Tunis.

OTTOMAN DEFEAT

The first great age of the Barbary corsairs was brought to an end by the Ottoman defeat at the Battle of Lepanto in 1571.

ISLAND FORTRESS

Djerba: another base for the fearsome Barbarossa brothers.

CHRISTIAN CORSAIRS

1522, Malta: the Knights Hospitaller were driven from Rhodes by the Barbary corsairs and Turks and made bases in Malta, Gozo and Tripoli. The rent paid to the Holy Roman Emperor was a single falcon each All Saints' Day.

CRUSADER STRONGHOLD

Until 1522, Rhodes: the stronghold of the Knights Hospitaller, an order of crusaders that turned to privateering and piracy, preying on Muslim shipping.

The Barbarossa Brothers

Flaming RED BEARDS

DARING

A SILVER FALSE ARM

Bold

Bloodthirsty

Gallant

THE BARBAROSSA BROTHERS WERE SOME OF THE MOST FEARSOME PIRATES OF THE MEDITERRANEAN SEA. THEY WERE BORN ON THE GREEK ISLAND OF LESBOS TO A TURKISH FATHER, AND BECAME SEAFARERS.

WANTED: 'Arūj and Khayr al-Dīn. **BORN:** c.1474. **ACTIVE:** 1495–1518, Mediterranean Sea. **DISTINGUISHING FEATURES:** flaming red beards, a silver false arm; bold, daring, gallant and bloodthirsty. **WANTED FOR:** raiding Christian settlements around the Mediterranean; seizing Christian ships.

TURNING PIRATE

It was a fateful day when Christian pirates captured the trading ship of 'Arūj Barbarossa on its way home from Tripoli. They killed his youngest brother, and held 'Arūj prisoner for almost three years in Turkey. Once free, he took his revenge by becoming the most feared privateer of the Mediterranean.

BROTHERS IN ARMS

An Ottoman prince gave 'Arūj a fleet of ships to fight against the Knights Hospitaller who had kidnapped him. He soon collected more ships, more allies – and more enemies. In 1503, his brother Khidr joined him. In exchange for a third of their booty, the Sultan of Tunisia gave them the fortress of La Goulette as their base.

With a licence as privateers, the brothers waged war on sea-going Europeans with terrifying ferocity, capturing ships and raiding the coasts of Spain and Italy. They were joined by other privateers.

RAIDERS OF LAND AND SEA

The brothers went from strength to strength, capturing 23 ships in a month in 1512, and even setting up their own gunpowder factory at La Goulette. They began campaigns inland, first seizing Algiers from the Spanish and then taking towns further from the sea.

'Arūj was now known as Barbarossa — meaning 'redbeard'. Barbarossa used his seaman's skills even on land, attaching sails to the cannons to transport them over the desert. He gave the lands to the Ottomans in exchange for galleys, cannons and the titles of governor of Algiers and chief governor of the Western Mediterranean.

But the Spanish fought back. After battling to defend their stronghold in Tlemcen for 20 days, the outnumbered corsairs were defeated and 'Arūj died in battle.

BARBAROSSA II

Khidr took over the name and role of Barbarossa – it's said he even dyed his beard red. He recaptured Tlemcen and drove the Knights Hospitaller from Rhodes. Now known as Khayr al-Dīn Barbarossa, he was made admiral of the Ottoman navy and governor of Rhodes: a grand move from pirate to statesman.

He still acted like a pirate, raiding and plundering towns and ships, but now also played a part in the great wars of Europe. He took the Greek islands, one after another, destroying most of Corfu and seizing nearly all the inhabitants as slaves. By the end of his career, he commanded a fleet of 210 ships and 30,000 Ottoman troops. He finally retired to a grand palace in Constantinople, where he died in 1546.

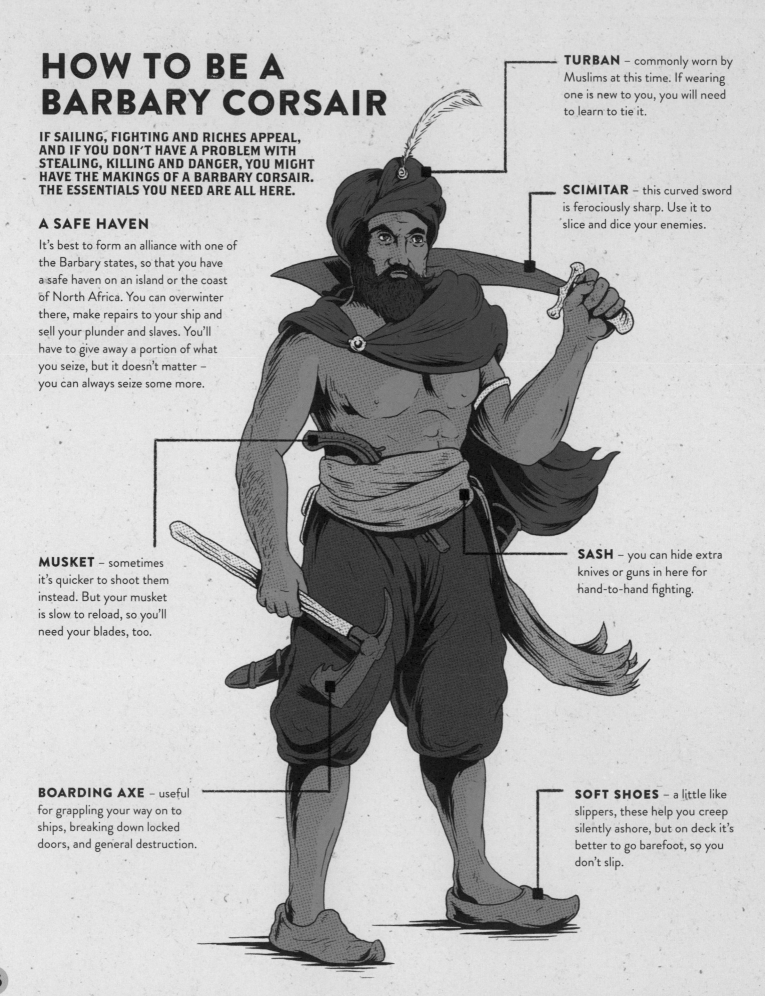

HOW TO BE A BARBARY CORSAIR

IF SAILING, FIGHTING AND RICHES APPEAL, AND IF YOU DON'T HAVE A PROBLEM WITH STEALING, KILLING AND DANGER, YOU MIGHT HAVE THE MAKINGS OF A BARBARY CORSAIR. THE ESSENTIALS YOU NEED ARE ALL HERE.

A SAFE HAVEN

It's best to form an alliance with one of the Barbary states, so that you have a safe haven on an island or the coast of North Africa. You can overwinter there, make repairs to your ship and sell your plunder and slaves. You'll have to give away a portion of what you seize, but it doesn't matter – you can always seize some more.

TURBAN – commonly worn by Muslims at this time. If wearing one is new to you, you will need to learn to tie it.

SCIMITAR – this curved sword is ferociously sharp. Use it to slice and dice your enemies.

MUSKET – sometimes it's quicker to shoot them instead. But your musket is slow to reload, so you'll need your blades, too.

SASH – you can hide extra knives or guns in here for hand-to-hand fighting.

BOARDING AXE – useful for grappling your way on to ships, breaking down locked doors, and general destruction.

SOFT SHOES – a little like slippers, these help you creep silently ashore, but on deck it's better to go barefoot, so you don't slip.

SAILS AND SLAVES

Obviously, you'll need a ship. It might be one you've captured, or maybe one you have had built. In the 1500s, the best is a galliot (half-galley). These small, fast ships have both sails and oars, rowed by slaves. They have a shallow draught, which means they can sail close to shore. If you can't find a crew, you can press some of your captives into serving with you. If they don't want to join you, threaten them with being sold into slavery.

Your pirate crew will have to trim the sails and navigate, so it's best to include some hardened sailors.

YOU DON'T NEED TO WORRY TOO MUCH ABOUT THE SLAVES. THEY WILL ROW BECAUSE THEY WILL BE WHIPPED TO DEATH IF THEY DON'T. YOU WILL NEED SLAVE-POWER WHEN THERE IS NO WIND, AND IN BATTLE TO MOVE YOUR SHIP AROUND QUICKLY.

GALLIOTS are easy to manoeuvre, so good for sudden attacks and speedy escapes.

DON'T GO DOWN TO THE LOWER DECK IF YOU CAN HELP IT — THE HEAT AND STENCH ARE INTOLERABLE. THE SLAVES RELIEVE THEMSELVES WHERE THEY SIT, BUT AS A CARING OWNER, YOU HAVE THE SHIP WASHED OUT EVERY COUPLE OF DAYS.

THE LOATHSOME LIFE OF A GALLEY SLAVE

WHILE A CORSAIR FACED A LIFE OF EXCITEMENT WITH THE POSSIBILITY OF RICHES, A GALLEY SLAVE COULD LOOK FORWARD TO A LIFE OF MISERY WITH A FAINT POSSIBILITY OF SURVIVAL.

SNATCHED!

Most slaves on corsair ships were captured in raids on the coast or from fishing boats or trading ships. Some were put to work at the oars straight away. They might sail six weeks or more before reaching land. Back on land, the captives were thrown into prisons called bagnos. They were often filthy, crowded and plagued by rats and insects.

At slave markets, men were sold to work as miners, labourers, or to serve as galley slaves. Those who had a trade or were educated often found better work, but they were still slaves. Women were often sold as domestic slaves.

Some slaves were eventually freed if their family or town could raise enough money, or they earned enough to buy their freedom. Many died in slavery.

SLAVES FOR ALL

It wasn't only the corsairs who used galley slaves. European navies also used captives and convicted criminals to row ships. For corsairs, this meant a captured galley came ready with slaves to row it.

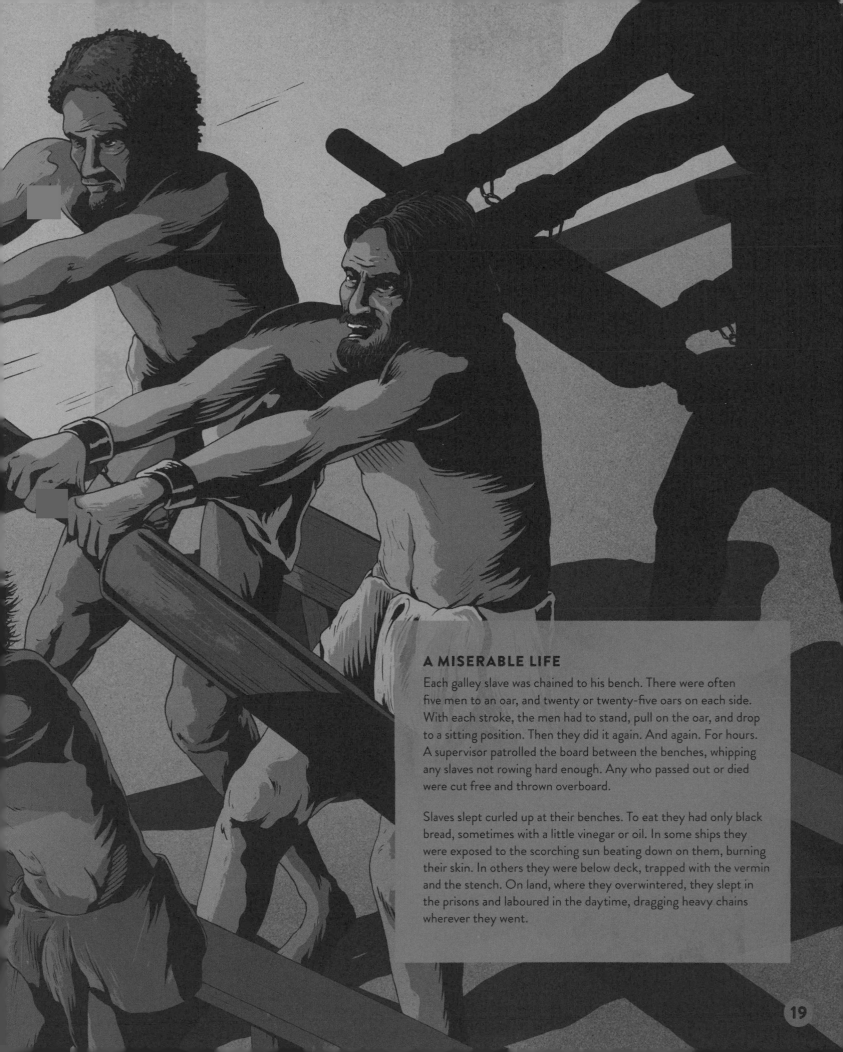

A MISERABLE LIFE

Each galley slave was chained to his bench. There were often five men to an oar, and twenty or twenty-five oars on each side. With each stroke, the men had to stand, pull on the oar, and drop to a sitting position. Then they did it again. And again. For hours. A supervisor patrolled the board between the benches, whipping any slaves not rowing hard enough. Any who passed out or died were cut free and thrown overboard.

Slaves slept curled up at their benches. To eat they had only black bread, sometimes with a little vinegar or oil. In some ships they were exposed to the scorching sun beating down on them, burning their skin. In others they were below deck, trapped with the vermin and the stench. On land, where they overwintered, they slept in the prisons and laboured in the daytime, dragging heavy chains wherever they went.

A SEA HELD TO RANSOM

THE EARLY CORSAIRS WERE LAWLESS ADVENTURERS, BUT PRIVATEERING GRADUALLY BECAME A MUCH MORE SERIOUS BUSINESS.

DEFINING BATTLES

The great age of the corsairs began in 1538 when Khayr-al-Dīn Barbarossa led the Ottoman navy to victory against a combined fleet of Christian European powers, led by Spain and Venice. The combined fleet was defeated off the shores of Preveza, and the Ottomans became the undisputed rulers of the sea.

Their triumph lasted just over 30 years, but ended with another sea battle in almost the same place. The Ottoman defeat at the Battle of Lepanto in 1571 ended the corsairs' involvement in campaigns with the navy – and they went back to pirating.

BIG BUSINESS

Corsair pirating became big business. People invested in corsairing, buying shares – just as investors buy shares in businesses today. They would put up money that was used to equip a ship and recruit a crew, and in return would gain a portion of the profit from seized goods and sold slaves. People from all walks of life invested in corsair businesses.

CAPTAIN OF THE SEA

As corsairing became more official, a special council, called the taife reisi (meaning 'board of captains'), emerged to regulate it. It was essentially a trade guild for pirates. It regulated recruitment, appointment of captains, planned routes and joint campaigns, organized the share and resale of booty and slaves and even elected a 'Captain of the Sea'. He ruled the guild and was chair of the corsairs' council.

In Algiers, corsair activity became the main source of income – the country ran on the pillaging of Christian ships and the money from ransoming and selling slaves.

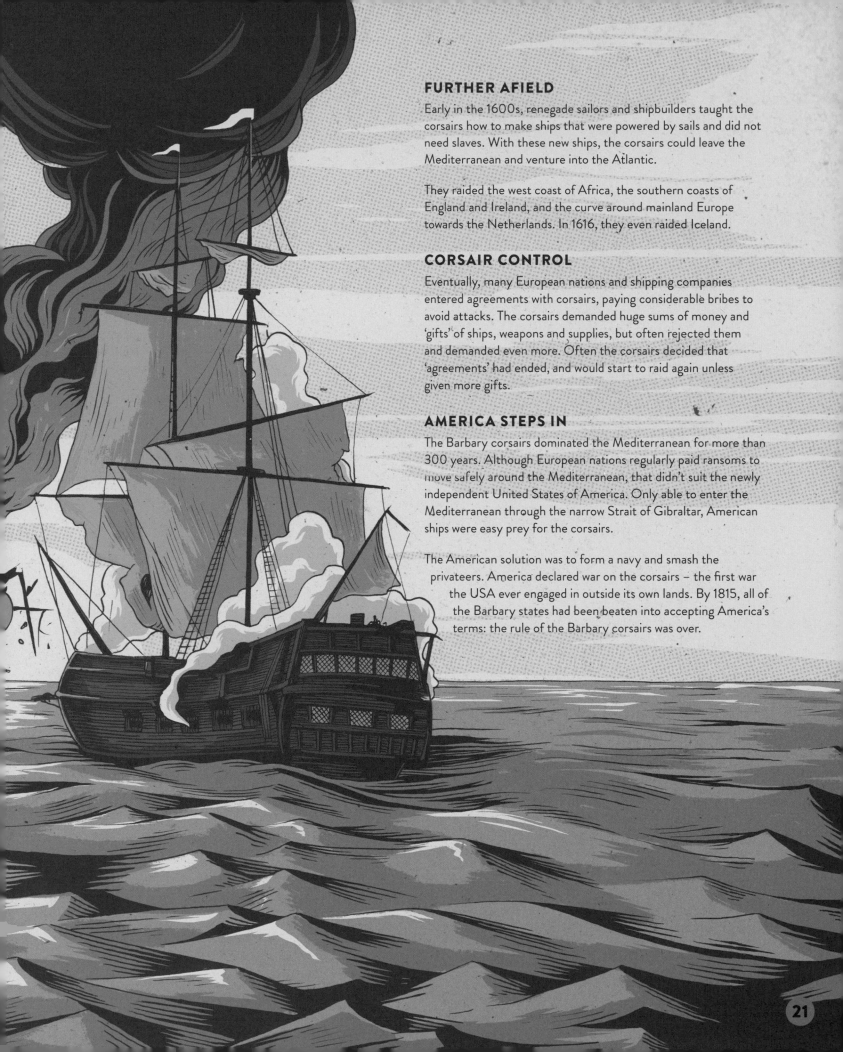

FURTHER AFIELD

Early in the 1600s, renegade sailors and shipbuilders taught the corsairs how to make ships that were powered by sails and did not need slaves. With these new ships, the corsairs could leave the Mediterranean and venture into the Atlantic.

They raided the west coast of Africa, the southern coasts of England and Ireland, and the curve around mainland Europe towards the Netherlands. In 1616, they even raided Iceland.

CORSAIR CONTROL

Eventually, many European nations and shipping companies entered agreements with corsairs, paying considerable bribes to avoid attacks. The corsairs demanded huge sums of money and 'gifts' of ships, weapons and supplies, but often rejected them and demanded even more. Often the corsairs decided that 'agreements' had ended, and would start to raid again unless given more gifts.

AMERICA STEPS IN

The Barbary corsairs dominated the Mediterranean for more than 300 years. Although European nations regularly paid ransoms to move safely around the Mediterranean, that didn't suit the newly independent United States of America. Only able to enter the Mediterranean through the narrow Strait of Gibraltar, American ships were easy prey for the corsairs.

The American solution was to form a navy and smash the privateers. America declared war on the corsairs – the first war the USA ever engaged in outside its own lands. By 1815, all of the Barbary states had been beaten into accepting America's terms: the rule of the Barbary corsairs was over.

PIRATE GOLD

THROUGHOUT HISTORY, PIRATES HAVE STOLEN WHATEVER THEY COULD FIND, BUT FROM THE 1500S, THEY REALLY DID HUNT DOWN SHIPS PACKED WITH TREASURE.

BLOOD AND GOLD

The gold and jewels came from South and Central America, and had been stolen from the local people by Spanish conquistadores ('conquering invaders').

After Christopher Columbus became the first European to reach the Bahamas in 1492, the Spanish sent more and more ships to explore the West Indies and then the mainland.

They stole gold first from the Aztec peoples of Mexico and then from the Inca empire in South America, claiming the lands and riches for Spain as they did so. The Spanish melted down the treasure to make coins and gold bars, which they sent to Spain across the Atlantic Ocean. But first they had to get past the pirates.

A LUCKY STRIKE

In 1523, a French corsair called Jean Fleury attacked three Spanish ships on their way back to Spain. The ships carried an astonishing cargo: three huge chests of gold bars, piles of gold dust, chests of pearls, emeralds and other gems. It also carried decorated Aztec armour, mosaic masks, brightly coloured feathered cloaks, exotic birds and animals – and even three live jaguars.

The discovery that the Spanish were shipping treasure back to Europe changed the world. First France, then England and later Holland licensed privateers to attack the ships. The great age of Caribbean piracy had begun.

BOOTY ROUTE

The main route for the treasure ships was through the Lesser Antilles to ports along the coastline of the Americas, then westwards to the north of Cuba and back to Europe.

THE TREASURE FLEET

Lone ships sailing the long distance from South America to Spain were easy targets, so the Spanish changed their strategy. From 1543, they sent two great convoys of around 100 ships each year to pick up the looted gold. They became known as the 'treasure fleet' and were protected by galleons or warships equipped with cannons.

A fleet of a hundred ships was too much for pirates to tackle, so instead they picked off ships travelling within the West Indies. As settlements grew up and trade flourished in the area, it was trading ships and ports that became the main – and easier – target for the pirates of the 1600s and 1700s.

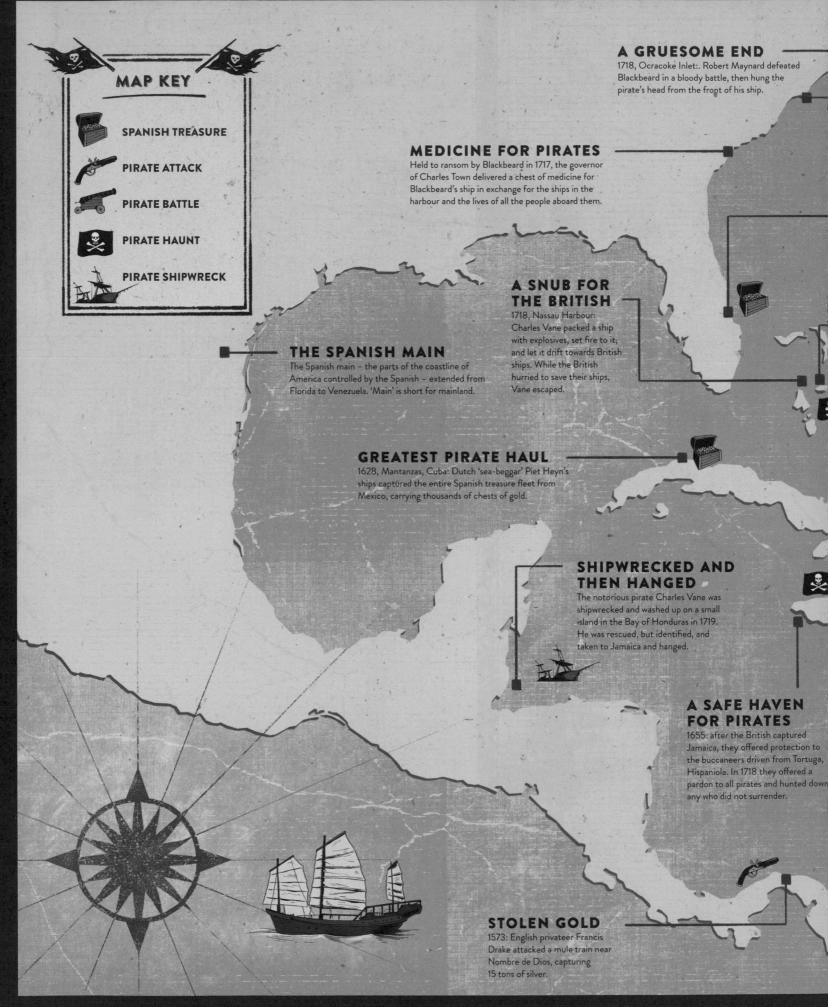

MAP KEY

SPANISH TREASURE

PIRATE ATTACK

PIRATE BATTLE

PIRATE HAUNT

PIRATE SHIPWRECK

A GRUESOME END

1718, Ocracoke Inlet:. Robert Maynard defeated Blackbeard in a bloody battle, then hung the pirate's head from the front of his ship.

MEDICINE FOR PIRATES

Held to ransom by Blackbeard in 1717, the governor of Charles Town delivered a chest of medicine for Blackbeard's ship in exchange for the ships in the harbour and the lives of all the people aboard them.

A SNUB FOR THE BRITISH

1718, Nassau Harbour: Charles Vane packed a ship with explosives, set fire to it, and let it drift towards British ships. While the British hurried to save their ships, Vane escaped.

THE SPANISH MAIN

The Spanish main – the parts of the coastline of America controlled by the Spanish – extended from Florida to Venezuela. 'Main' is short for mainland.

GREATEST PIRATE HAUL

1628, Mantanzas, Cuba: Dutch 'sea-beggar' Piet Heyn's ships captured the entire Spanish treasure fleet from Mexico, carrying thousands of chests of gold.

SHIPWRECKED AND THEN HANGED

The notorious pirate Charles Vane was shipwrecked and washed up on a small island in the Bay of Honduras in 1719. He was rescued, but identified, and taken to Jamaica and hanged.

A SAFE HAVEN FOR PIRATES

1655: after the British captured Jamaica, they offered protection to the buccaneers driven from Tortuga, Hispaniola. In 1718 they offered a pardon to all pirates and hunted down any who did not surrender.

STOLEN GOLD

1573: English privateer Francis Drake attacked a mule train near Nombre de Dios, capturing 15 tons of silver.

PIRATES OF THE CARIBBEAN

THE RICHES OF THE NEW WORLD OFFERED UNTOLD TEMPTATION TO SAILORS BOLD ENOUGH TO ATTACK THE BOOTY-LADEN SHIPS OF THE SPANISH TREASURE FLEET.

MAROONED

Blackbeard grounded two of his ships and marooned many of his own men at Topsail Inlet. It might have been an accident or he might have done it to increase his share of the loot.

TREASURE WRECK

1715, Vero Beach: of 12 ships in the 1715 Spanish treasure fleet, 11 were wrecked in a hurricane a week after leaving Cuba, killing 1,000 sailors. Pieces of the treasure are still being found today.

THE PIRATES' REPUBLIC

1706 to 1718: Nassau on New Providence Island was under pirate rule. It was a safe haven where they could mend their ships, trade, party and rest.

FIRST STRIKE FOR GOLD!

The secret of Spanish gold shipments was discovered in 1523 when privateer Jean Fleury attacked three ships heading home with a haul of Aztec treasure.

BUCCANEERS' STRONGHOLD

c. 1630: fleeing Hispaniola, buccaneers set up a base on nearby Tortuga island. Their stronghold, the Fort de Rocher, was stormed by the Spanish in 1654.

A GRISLY PRIZE

Around 1572: French privateer Jean Bontemps and 70 followers tried to raid the island of Curaçao off Venezuela, but heavy rain prevented them using their guns. Bontemps was killed, and his head was cut off and taken to Hispaniola as a trophy.

CARIBBEAN SEA

HANGED ON THE SHORE

Many pirates were hanged at Gallows Point, Jamaica, including Calico Jack and Charles Vane. The swinging corpses were often bound in chains and hung at the entrance to the harbour, a gruesome warning to other pirates.

A SELF-MAROONING PIRATE

Pursued by HMS *Eagle*, the pirate George Lowther managed to slip ashore at Blanquilla, but it did him little good: his dead body was found there a few days later.

TREASURE PACKED AND READY TO SAIL

The Spanish treasure fleet picked up plundered gold and treasure at Cartagena, Nombre de Dios and Porto Bello before shipping it back to Spain.

DARING DECEPTION

Maracaibo: pirate Henry Morgan deceived Spanish pursuers by disguising a near-empty ship as his flagship – drilling holes and fitting logs as 'cannon', and standing wooden figures on the deck. He sailed it towards three Spanish warships and blew it up with gunpowder.

THE HUNT FOR TREASURE

AS SOON AS EUROPEAN NATIONS REALIZED THAT SPANISH GALLEONS WERE CROSSING THE ATLANTIC, PACKED WITH PRICELESS TREASURE, THEY SET ABOUT SEIZING IT.

PICK A PIRATE

First came French corsairs, because the French and Spanish were already enemies. Then the English fell out with Spain, and English privateers – called 'sea-dogs' – joined in. When England and Spain made peace, the Dutch sent their privateers, called sea beggars. But when a country made peace with Spain, its privateers simply turned to piracy for their own profit.

SALTY SEA-DOGS

The sea-dogs were English privateers, licensed by Queen Elizabeth I to prey on Spanish ships, and backed by fleets of warships. For some sea-dogs, privateering was just one of their interests. Privateer John Hawkins also started the terrible trade that took slaves from Africa and traded them in the Caribbean for gold, rum, spices and sugar that was then sold back in England.

Navigator Sir Francis Drake was known as 'the Queen's pirate' as he was a favourite at court and hugely successful at snatching Spanish plunder. In 1573, he ambushed a mule train near Nombre de Dios, Panama, and carried away 15 tons of silver. He later commanded a fleet with hundreds of soldiers.

DUTCH SUCCESS

The most daring assault was led by Dutch privateer Piet Heyn. In 1628, he captured the entire Spanish treasure fleet, with treasure worth 12 million Dutch guilders – nearly $400,000,000 in today's money. Most ships surrendered quickly, and no Spanish sailors were killed.

BARBECUE BUCCANEERS

Also attacking the Spanish in the Caribbean were buccaneers, a mixed bunch from many nations. They were originally criminals, runaway slaves, unemployed plantation workers or others from the island of Hispaniola. They hunted wild pigs and cattle, and were tough and heavily armed. They were called buccaneers because they smoked their meat on a grill over a fire, rather like a barbecue, which was called a 'buccan' by the native people of Hispaniola.

FROM PIG-HUNTERS TO PIRATES

The Spanish tried to drive the buccaneers away. The men, in turn, began attacking Spanish ships. A band of buccaneers sailed to the rocky island of Tortuga and built a fort stronghold that lasted until five Spanish warships destroyed it in 1654.

The buccaneers then moved to Jamaica, an island captured by the British in 1655. The British welcomed them, and gave them 'letters of marque', making them official privateers.

Blackheard

FIERCE and WILD

A Devil INCARNATE

IF EVER THERE WAS A FEARSOME PIRATE, IT WAS BLACKBEARD. HIS APPEARANCE WAS TERRIFYING, AND HIS RUTHLESS FEROCITY WAS DIRECTED AGAINST HIS OWN CREW AS WELL AS HIS ENEMIES.

BORN: c.1680, Bristol, England. **ACTIVE:** 1717–1718, Caribbean.
DISTINGUISHING FEATURES: 'So fierce and wild ... that imagination cannot form an idea of a Fury, from Hell, to look more frightful... Some of his frolics of wickedness were so extravagant, as if he aimed at making the men believe he was a devil incarnate.' (*A General History of the Pyrates*, 1794)

FROM PRIVATEER TO PIRATE

When Britain made peace with Spain (again) in 1714, many privateers who had made a living preying on Spanish shipping turned to piracy. Edward Teach, known as Blackbeard, was one of them. He joined a pirate ship in New Providence, the Bahamas. By 1716, he was captain of a sloop (a small, fast, single-masted ship). The next year he captured a slave ship and renamed it *Queen Anne's Revenge*. Fitted with 40 guns, it became his flagship, feared throughout the Caribbean.

A TERRIFYING PROSPECT

Blackbeard knew that frightening his victims was half the battle. He wore his huge black beard in plaits tied with ribbons. In battle, he set fire to fuses of hemp cord tucked under his hat, so that clouds of black smoke billowed around his head. He carried at least three pairs of pistols, as well as knives and cutlasses.

Known for his cruelty, Blackbeard would as soon cut off a finger wearing a ring as wait for the owner to give him the jewel. He even shot his second in command, Israel Hands, saying he needed to remind his men to fear him.

MEDICAL EMERGENCY

Once, short of medicine on his ship, Blackbeard sailed to Charles Town, Carolina. He threatened to burn all the ships in the harbour, kill everyone on board, and send their heads to the governor unless he was brought the medicines he needed. With moments to go, and the hostages ready to hang, the medicine arrived.

HUNTED DOWN

In 1718, Blackbeard accepted a pardon offered by the British to all pirates. But first he ran two of his ships aground and marooned about 25 men on an island, leaving them to die. Maybe he thought he'd have a larger share of the loot that way.

Despite the pardon, the governor of Virginia sent Lieutenant Robert Maynard in pursuit of Blackbeard. He tracked Blackbeard to Ocracoke Inlet. Hiding his men below deck, Maynard tricked Blackbeard into thinking the crew were all dead. But when Blackbeard's men boarded Maynard's sloop, the hidden crew came out fighting. In bloody hand-to-hand combat with Maynard, Blackbeard survived five pistol shots and twenty slashes with a cutlass before dying. Maynard sliced off Blackbeard's head and hung it from the bowsprit of his ship.

LIVE LIKE A PIRATE

LIFE FOR ALL SAILORS WAS HARD, BUT FOR PIRATES IT WAS EVEN HARDER. IF YOU WANT TO BE A PIRATE, PREPARE FOR SOME TERRIBLE TIMES.

PIRATE JOB DESCRIPTION

You'll have to carry out all the usual tasks of sailing a ship, but also be good at fighting with cutlasses, pistols and knives. A pirate who can't fight doesn't live long. You need to keep your weapons clean and in good working order – forgetting could cost you your life.

THE GOOD, THE BAD AND THE BUGLY

Food can be good – or horrid. After a shore visit, you have fresh food and fruit, clean water and good rum. But after only a day or two at sea in hot weather, it soon spoils. You might be lucky and find food on a captured ship, but a bad run will see you reduced to eating rotting meat, bread and fruit, or nothing but ship's biscuits and stinking water crawling with bugs. Rum and beer might actually be healthier!

On bad days, the only food is hard tack – rock-hard biscuit that has to be soaked in water to become edible. You might have a little salted pork, beef or horsemeat left. If you can catch a live turtle, that makes a good meal – and it stays fresh if you keep it alive in the ship's hold until you want to cook it.

PIRATE PONG

You can't be too fussy about smells as a pirate. There are no toilets, your shipmates don't wash, and there are lots of you, crammed together in the boiling hot, wet air of the ship.

The very bottom of the ship has its own smelly problem. This is the bilge, where seawater that has slopped and leaked into the ship collects. Some poor crew member has to keep pumping out the water – and all the furry, crawly, slimy things that have died in there.

You'll also have to use the 'jardine' sometime, so don't be shy. It's a hole in a plank that juts out over the sea and it's the nearest thing to a toilet you will find.

PIRATES AND OTHER PESTS

It's pretty crowded on the ship. Not only are there lots of pirates – enough to overpower the crew of a larger ship – but there are other pesky passengers: rats, fleas, lice, spiders, scorpions and cockroaches.

ARTICLES OF AGREEMENT

1. Every man shall obey the orders of the captain. Every man in the crew shall have a share in all treasure seized. The captain shall have one-and-a-half times the normal share. The master, carpenter, boatswain and gunner shall have one-and-a-quarter share.

2. If any man tries to run away, he shall be marooned with one bottle of gunpowder, one bottle of water, one pistol, and a shot for the pistol.

3. If any man steals anything from the crew worth more than a piece of eight (a silver coin), he shall be marooned or shot.

4. Any man who signs the Articles of another pirate ship without consent will be punished, as the captain and company (the crew) think fit.

5. Any man who strikes another member of the company shall suffer 39 lashes on his bare back.

6. Any man who smokes tobacco in the hold (inside the ship), or carries a lighted candle not in a lantern, shall suffer 39 lashes.

7. Any man who does not keep his weapons clean and fit shall lose his share (see Article One), and suffer any other punishment the captain and company think fit.

8. If any man shall lose a joint (a hand or foot) in battle, he shall have 400 pieces of eight; if a limb, 800 pieces.

PIRATE PUNISHMENTS

PIRATES COULD BE BRUTAL AND RUTHLESS TO THEIR VICTIMS, BUT THEIR OWN CREWS FARED NO BETTER IF THEY BROKE THE ARTICLES OF AGREEMENT. HERE ARE SOME PUNISHMENTS YOU'D REALLY WANT TO AVOID.

FLOGGING

Pirates lashed offenders with a whip, rope or 'cat o'nine tails'. The 'cat' was made from a piece of rope with its nine strands unwound, knotted at the ends and then covered in tar. The hard ends cut skin to ribbons. But in actual fact, flogging was less common on pirate ships than in regular navies.

KEEL-HAULING

The pirate to be punished was bound and attached to a rope, then dragged beneath the ship from one end to the other, or side-to-side. If he didn't drown, the razor-sharp shells of barnacles growing on the hull would cut his flesh to ribbons. It was a terrible punishment, and often deadly.

SWEATING

Sometimes the captain of a captured ship would be punished by 'sweating'. He was taken below decks, and a circle of candles or lanterns was lit. Then the man had to run around naked while all the pirates poked and jabbed at him with swords, knives and needles until he was exhausted and bleeding. It wasn't intended to kill the captain, but to humiliate him.

MAROONING

The worst punishment of all was marooning. The pirate was abandoned on a small island without food or shelter. He was sometimes given a pistol and one or two rounds of shot, and maybe a bottle of water. He could choose to shoot himself or die slowly of hunger, starvation and the heat. The only chance of escape was if a passing ship rescued him.

CRUELTY BACKFIRES

Charles Vane was a notoriously cruel pirate. He cheated his own men, tortured the crews of captured ships, and killed them after promising mercy. Sailors were so afraid of encountering him that they stopped trading around the Bahamas in 1718. In 1719, Vane's ship was shipwrecked and he washed up on an uninhabited island in the Bay of Honduras. A ship came by, but the captain, Holford, was a former pirate and recognized him, refusing to take him on board. Another ship did pick him up, but unluckily for Vane, Holford came aboard and spotted him. He revealed his identity, and the captain took Vane to Jamaica, where he was hanged.

MOSES'S LAW

Being sentenced to 'Moses's law' meant being flogged exactly 39 times. It refers to the maximum amount of lashes allowed in Jewish Law in the Old Testament of the Bible. So 39 lashes was regarded as a severe punishment.

Mary Read

Anne Bonny

Both very profligate cursing and swearing much

BORN: c.1690, England (Read); c.1700, Ireland (Bonny). **ACTIVE:** 1718–1720, Caribbean. **DISTINGUISHING FEATURES:** 'Both very profligate, cursing and swearing much'. (*A General History of the Pyrates*, 1794). **WANTED FOR:** piracy in the Caribbean under the captaincy of Calico Jack.

MARY READ

Mary Read was born in England to a poor, single mother who dressed her as a boy. Her mother pretended Mary was her dead son so that her ex-mother-in-law would give her financial support. Aged 13, Read became a foot soldier in Belgium. She fell in love with another soldier and they married, but soon he died. Dressing as a man again, she set off to the West Indies. Her ship was captured by English pirates and she agreed to join them.

ANNE BONNY

Anne Bonny's father, while living in London, disguised her as a boy. When it came out that she was his illegitimate daughter, he took her to Carolina in America. There, Anne married a penniless sailor. The couple went to the Bahamas to find work, but a famous pirate, 'Calico Jack' Rackham, persuaded Bonny to leave her husband and go to sea with him.

PIRATING TOGETHER

There were over 2,000 pirates operating around the Caribbean, yet the only two known to be women ended up on Calico Jack's ship, possibly after Jack attacked the ship Read was on. The women were as fierce and dedicated as the men, handling guns, gunpowder and cutlasses. Both swore and called for the murder of passengers and crew of boats they attacked as often as their male shipmates.

CALICO JACK

John Rackham was known as Calico Jack because of his colourful cotton clothes (calico is a kind of cloth). He met and later married Anne Bonny and they had a child. Read and Bonny revealed to Jack that Read was also a woman after he became jealous of Bonny's friendship with what seemed to be a pretty young pirate boy.

HOW DID THEY GET AWAY WITH IT?

Many young men and teenage boys worked on ships, and all wore loose clothing and long hair, often tied back or plaited. Read and Bonny were used to male clothing and were active, strong women. It was not too difficult for them to carry off their disguises.

AN END ASHORE

In 1720, Pirate Hunter Captain Jonathan Barnet hunted down and attacked Calico's ship off the coast of Jamaica. Bonny and Read fought the attackers while most of the other members of the crew hid below, surrendered or were too drunk to fight.

All members of the crew except Bonny and Read were hanged at Gallows Point, Jamaica. The two women were spared because they were pregnant. Read died in prison from fever in 1721, but no one knows what became of Bonny. There is no record of either her execution or her release.

'Had you fought like a man, you need not have been hanged like a dog.'

These are said to be Bonny's last words to Calico Jack, before he was hanged.

PIRATES RULE!

PIRATES NEED A SAFE HAVEN WHERE THEY CAN REPAIR THEIR SHIPS, BUY SUPPLIES AND TRADE THEIR PLUNDER. IN THE BAHAMAS, THE ISLAND OF NEW PROVIDENCE WAS SO OVERRUN WITH PIRATES IT WAS CALLED THE PIRATES' REPUBLIC.

FROM ORDER TO CHAOS

In 1696, the pirate Henry Avery came to Nassau, New Providence, and bribed its English governor to let him trade his loot there. Soon, Nassau became a safe base for other pirates.

In 1703 and 1706, French and Spanish fleets attacked the island and most of the English settlers fled. With no official governor, the pirates took over and ran the island as their own republic. It became a lawless place of drinking, gambling and violence.

At one point there were a thousand pirates to only a hundred ordinary, peaceful islanders. The pirates on the island, including Benjamin Hornigold and Henry Jennings, formed a fearsome group called the Flying Gang.

PIRATE HAVOC – AND REVENGE

The Flying Gang became so powerful that it could attack the British navy. It caused such havoc that eventually the British king, George I, sent a new governor to take charge.

Woodes Rogers arrived in 1718, bringing seven ships and a royal pardon for any pirate who would give up piracy. Many did so or pretended to. One who did give up was Hornigold, who was employed by Rogers to hunt persistent pirates.

It was a cunning move: Hornigold knew the pirates' ways and could hunt them better than any navy man. He quickly caught ten of his former allies, and nine were hanged in December 1718. That marked the return of British rule and the end of the pirates' republic.

DIE LIKE A PIRATE!

Often, condemned pirates were hanged and buried between the points of high and low tide. Sometimes the bodies of famous pirates, such as Calico Jack Rackham, were strapped into a metal cage, or bound in chains then hung from a gibbet (wooden frame), at the entrance to a harbour.

There, the body would sway in the wind, its chains creaking, as it slowly rotted away. As the body fell apart, or was eaten by gulls, there was nothing to bury. That meant the pirate's soul could not find rest after death – a terrible punishment for a superstitious pirate.

A WHOLE NEW WORLD

IN 1497 THE PORTUGUESE EXPLORER VASCO DA GAMA SAILED AROUND THE SOUTHERN TIP OF AFRICA INTO THE INDIAN OCEAN. HE FOUND A SEA BUSTLING WITH TRADE – AND WITH PIRATES.

PIRATES WITH A PLAN

Indian pirates from Malabar had been at large in the Indian Ocean from at least as early as the 1290s. When fishing was poor, whole families set off in fleets of around 100 boats. They spread out, making a net of boats to trap merchant ships, then alerted each other with smoke signals to close in on them.

If they suspected their victims of swallowing precious jewels or pearls, the pirates forced them to swallow a sour paste of the spice tamarind and seawater. It made them violently sick. Hardened pirates weren't squeamish about picking jewels out of vomit.

ATTACKING THE TRADE ROUTES

In the 1600s, fierce Indian pirates were already operating from the coast south of Mumbai using light, quick boats called grabs (from *ghorab,* Arabic for 'raven'). They worked in small groups, darting out from hidden inlets to attack passing ships.

NORTH AMERICAN PIRATES

Many of the European pirates who were active in the Indian Ocean had already been operating in North America and the Caribbean. Wealthy Americans provided money to fund pirating trips and made a profit from the activity. In 1695, the governor of New York was happy for pirates to land at the port in exchange for a 'gift' of £700.

A MAGNET FOR PIRATES

After Vasco da Gama's trip to the Indian Ocean, the Portuguese set up trade routes to India. But from 1600, Dutch and then British ships joined in. Each country set up its own East India Company to trade in India and eastern Asia.

Pirates followed the trade in valuable silks, spices and timber, all of which was paid for in gold and silver. There was soon a dangerous mix of European and local trading ships, local Indian and African pirates, and European and North American pirates. The sea was seething with pirate activity.

TRADING AND RAIDING

Pirates preferred to seize ships on their way to Asia, when they were full of gold and silver, rather than plunder them for the goods they carried on their way back. Indeed, they had so little use for things like extravagant silks that one pirate ship replaced its worn-out canvas sails with silk sails.

A RICH PRIZE

1693: Thomas Tew captured a 300-man
Moghul ship sailing through the Red Sea,
taking £100,000 worth of gold and silver.
Each man claimed £1,200–£3,000 – more
than most could expect to earn in a lifetime.

SANGA

The fearsome Indian Sanganian
pirates sailed off the coast of
Gujarat. They took drugs to make
themselves wild and crazed, and let
their long hair flow loose as a sign
that they would give no mercy.

A NARROW SQUEEZE

Pirates could easily pick off
ships as they entered or left the
Bab-el-Mandeb, a narrow strait
(passage) joining the Red Sea
and Indian Ocean.

A MIGHTY BATTLE

1695: Henry Avery, Thomas
Tew and three other pirate
captains attacked 25 Moghul
ships heading for the Red
Sea. The pirates won, but
Tew was disembowelled by a
cannonball and died.

MAP KEY

 PIRATE HAUNT

PIRATE ATTACK

PIRATE BATTLE

 GHOST TOWN

KANHOJI ANGRE AND THE MARATHAS

The Indian Marathas, under Kanhoji Angre and
then his son Tulaji, demanded ships pay to cross
their waters and harassed those who would not.
The British considered them pirates.

THE END OF THE GOLDEN AGE

Around 1728: pirate strongholds in
Réunion and Mauritius had been
destroyed and actions by several
governments meant that the
Golden Age of piracy came
gradually to an end.

ALL ABOARD FOR PIRACY

1696: to replace crew killed by cholera as
he sailed round the tip of Africa, Scottish
sailor William Kidd had to take on extra men.
Many turned out to be pirates and probably
drove him along the path to piracy.

INDIAN
OCEAN

'GONE TO MADAGASCAR FOR LYMES'

Madagascar became a key stopping point
on the 'Pirate Round' (a route from the west
Atlantic, around the southern tip of Africa
and on to targets in Asia), offering a safe
haven and fresh food.

MAROONED ON MAURITIUS

1720: Pirate Edward England was
marooned with three of his men on
Mauritius for four months, when his
crew replaced him as captain. The four
escaped after building a small boat.

INTO A NEW SEA

1497: when Vasco da Gama sailed around the Cape
of Good Hope at the southernmost tip of Africa,
he entered a sea new to Europeans, already plied by
Indian, African and Arab traders and pirates.

FIGHTING BACK

1670s: the president of the British East India Company in Surat employed privateers to try to stop pirates who were attacking the company's ships.

PIRATES LONG AGO

1290: Marco Polo encountered pirates off the coast of India who worked in groups. After looting a ship, they let it go so that it might bring more plunder on another trip.

SEVERNDROOG FORTRESS

1755: William James, leading ships of the East India Company fleet, attacked Tulaji Angre's pirate fortress at Severndroog (Suvarnadurg) south of Mumbai and destroyed it.

LIFE AT SEA

The Orang Laut pirates from the Spice Islands had no land base and spent their lives on boats, with their wives and children.

HEAD-HUNTING PIRATES

The so-called Sea Dayaks of Borneo were said to be head-hunters (pirates who collected the heads of enemies as trophies). They preyed on boats travelling between Hong Kong and Singapore. They were brutally crushed by White Rajah James Brooke and a Malaysian army in the 1840s.

AFRICA AND MADAGASCAR

AT THE SAME TIME AS BLACKBEARD AND ANNE BONNY AND MARY READ WERE WREAKING HAVOC IN THE CARIBBEAN, PIRATES SUCH AS WILLIAM KIDD AND HENRY AVERY WERE PLAGUING THE INDIAN OCEAN AND BEYOND.

ROBBERY IN THE INDIAN OCEAN

PEACE BETWEEN BRITAIN AND SPAIN PUT MANY PRIVATEERS OUT OF WORK IN 1713. SO MANY AMERICAN AND EUROPEAN PIRATES HEADED FOR ASIA, AS NEW TRADE ROUTES OPENED UP IN THE INDIAN OCEAN AND BEYOND.

THE 'PIRATE ROUND'

The best route to sail, for a good chance of booty, was the 'Pirate Round' across the Atlantic to Africa, around the southern tip and up to the island of Madagascar (a good place to stock up on supplies or pick up extra crew), then off across the Indian Ocean. This roughly followed the route of East India Company traders.

The 'Round' route was pioneered by Thomas Tew, who set sail in 1692 with letters of marque from the governor of the Bahamas to destroy a French trading post on the West African coast. On the way, he suggested to his crew that they turn pirate and make a profit from their bravery instead of serving the governor's interests. His crew's famous response was, "A gold chain or a wooden leg, we'll stand with you!"

After a few months, they intercepted the treasure ship of the Moghul (Indian) emperor sailing from India to Arabia. The ship surrendered without a fight, and Tew shared over £100,000-worth of gold, silver jewels, silks and ivory with his crew. He was treated as a hero on his return to New York.

He set off on a second voyage in 1694, but it did not go as well. He joined forces with other pirates, including Henry Avery, and they attacked a convoy of 25 Moghul ships. The mission was a success, but not for Tew – he died after having his innards blown out by a cannonball.

A PIRATE'S ISLAND

The island of Madagascar, off the east coast of Africa, became a haven where a pirate ship could moor for cleaning and repair, trade booty and stock up on food.

By 1685, the pirate Adam Baldridge had set up a base on St Mary's, a tiny island off the north coast of Madagascar, after fleeing Jamaica where he was wanted for murder. He sold supplies to pirates at very high prices and lived like a prince on the proceeds. Baldridge was driven out in 1697, but in 1715 James Plantain started a new base at nearby Ranter's Point.

HOW TO ATTACK A SHIP

IF YOU WANT TO LAUNCH A PIRATE ATTACK, YOU NEED TO BE WELL ARMED, FIERCE AND RUTHLESS – BUT DON'T FIGHT UNLESS YOU HAVE TO!

BE SCARY

Your best weapons as a pirate are surprise and fear. If you have a reputation for being cruel, and your victims are convinced you will kill or torture them, you won't need to do it – they will hand over their jewels, their cargo, and even their ship without putting up a fight.

But if you have to attack...

You can launch a raid from a huge warship or some captured native canoes. Whichever you have, speed and surprise give you the edge.

1. Do you have a fast ship? Try dragging ropes in the water behind it to slow it down. At the last minute, haul the ropes in and your ship will speed up.

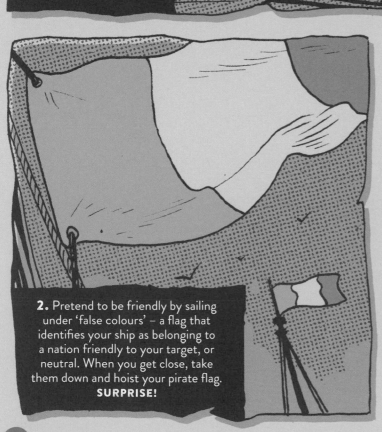

2. Pretend to be friendly by sailing under 'false colours' – a flag that identifies your ship as belonging to a nation friendly to your target, or neutral. When you get close, take them down and hoist your pirate flag. **SURPRISE!**

3. If you plan to give no quarter (mercy), hoist a red flag – everyone knows what it means.

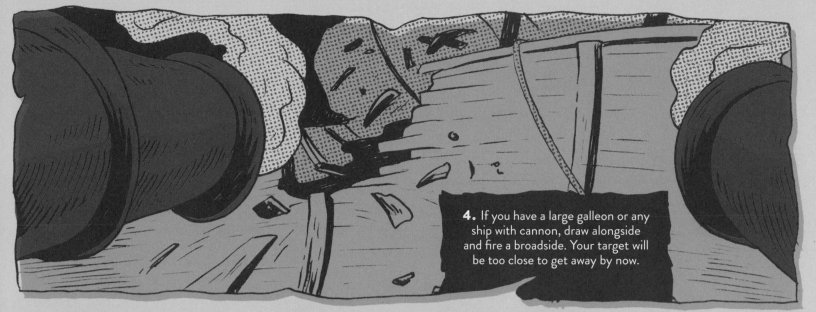

4. If you have a large galleon or any ship with cannon, draw alongside and fire a broadside. Your target will be too close to get away by now.

5. If you only have small boats, pull alongside and have your best marksmen shoot key members of the crew.

6. Do you have a large crew? Hide most of them below decks until they are needed.

7. Make sure you have an easily recognizable pirate flag to strike fear into the hearts of all sailors.

MIND THE SHIP

If you want to add the ship you are attacking to your fleet, don't destroy it by firing a broadside. Instead, have your pirates shoot key members of the crew, fire through ropes holding up the sails, or even fell a mast with a single cannonball. It's easier to replace a mast than patch huge, gaping holes in the hull.

COMMUNICATED in Welsh

A gallant figure

BLACK BART

BARTHOLOMEW ROBERTS WAS THE MOST SUCCESSFUL PIRATE OF HIS AGE, IN TERMS OF NUMBER OF SHIPS CAPTURED. BUT BLACK BART, AS HE WAS KNOWN, WAS A RELUCTANT CONVERT TO PIRACY.

BORN: c.1682, Wales. **ACTIVE:** 1719–1722, west coast of Africa and the Americas. **DISTINGUISHING FEATURES:** 'A gallant figure ... being dressed in a rich crimson damask waistcoat and breeches, a red feather in his hat, a gold chain round his neck, with a diamond cross hanging to it, a sword in his hand, and two pairs of pistols slung over his shoulders'. (*A General History of the Pyrates*, 1794). **WANTED FOR:** Piracy in the Atlantic Ocean.

Bartholomew Roberts was working as third mate on board a slave ship when it was attacked by pirates in 1719. He was forced, against his wishes, to join the pirates. The captain, Howell Davis, was a Welshman like Roberts, and the two could communicate in Welsh without others being able to understand. Davis was impressed by Roberts's navigation skills, too.

Only six weeks later, when Davis was killed in an ambush, Roberts was chosen to replace him. He accepted, saying that as he had already "dipped his hands in muddy water, and must be a pirate", he might as well be in charge. His first act was to avenge the death of Davis. It cemented the crew's loyalty to him.

A FINE CAREER

After waiting nine weeks off the coast of Brazil for a ship to attack, they were about to give up when 42 Portuguese ships stuffed full of treasure appeared. It was the first of many successful attacks for Roberts.

Over the next two years, Roberts and his men preyed on shipping and land along the American coast from Brazil to Newfoundland in Canada. His attacks were so frequent he almost put an end to trading by sea in the West Indies.

In one cheeky attack he approached a French ship under friendly colours and offered advice about the whereabouts of the pirate Bartholomew Roberts! Once alongside, he attacked and seized the ship. The governor of Martinique, who was on board, was hanged from the yardarm.

TIME'S UP

With shipping scarce in the West Indies, Roberts crossed the Atlantic to continue his plundering off the African coast.

All went well until February 1722, when a British navy ship, the HMS *Swallow*, found Roberts with three of his ships at Cape Lopez in west Africa. When HMS *Swallow* attacked, many of the pirate crew were drunk and incapable of defending their ship, as they had been celebrating the capture of another vessel.

Roberts, who always dressed in his finest clothes before an engagement, was shot in the throat and died. Honouring his wishes, the pirate crew quickly wrapped his body in the ship's flag, weighted it, and buried him at sea. His body has never been found.

It's said that Bartholomew Roberts drank no rum, preferring just tea.

SHIP AHOY!

PIRATE SHIPS NEEDED TO BE FAST AND MANOEUVRABLE, BUT THEY OFTEN DIDN'T LAST LONG. LUCKILY, IT WAS EASY TO CAPTURE A NEW SHIP FROM A TRADER OR EVEN A NAVY FLEET.

XEBEC
Used by the Barbary corsairs and rarely ever seen outside the Mediterranean Sea, a xebec had two or three masts with triangular sails, and oars worked by galley slaves. The boat was shallow, so could move quickly and travel in shallow water.

SCHOONER
Commonly used in the North Atlantic and around the Caribbean, schooners usually had two masts, each with a large sail. They were light and nimble, with a narrow hull and shallow draught so they could lurk in shallow coves and then dart out. But they were large enough to carry enough guns and pirates for a serious attack.

HOW FAST IS THAT SHIP?
The speed of a ship is measured in knots. Sailors (or pirates) time how quickly a knotted rope is pulled from a reel into the water by the ship moving forwards. Knots are spaced 14.4 m apart, and if one knot passes in 28 seconds, the ship is said to be going at a speed of 1 knot – equal to one nautical mile – or 1.85 km per hour.

SLOOP
Another shallow-draughted fast ship, a sloop had a single mast. Used mostly in the Caribbean and Atlantic, it had a top speed of 12 knots and could outrun most other ships.

BOATS USED BY THE WOKOU PIRATES AROUND CHINA AND KOREA OFTEN HAD A MAST THAT COULD BE LOWERED TO USE AS A BRIDGE FOR BOARDING THE SHIPS THEY ATTACKED.

GALLEON

This was a large warship that was usually the victim of pirate attacks rather than a pirate vessel. The Spanish used galleons to move treasure from the Caribbean to Europe. They were heavy and slow, but excellent for transporting cargo. Galleons had three masts, and two or three decks. Large numbers of heavy cannon made them hard to attack at sea.

JUNK

Used by Chinese pirates and merchants, junks have flat bottoms and a rudder that make them easy to steer. They have two or three masts with square sails made from bamboo, rattan or grass.

OR YOU COULD BUY A SHIP...

Stede Bonnet was unusual. A wealthy landowner born in Barbados, he bought a ship (rather than stole it) and set off for a life of piracy in 1717.

He had no knowledge of sailing or piracy and paid his crew wages rather than a share of treasure. He was injured in an encounter with a Spanish warship almost before he started.

Bonnet soon fell in with Blackbeard, but after a while Blackbeard took Bonnet's ship and most of his crew. Bonnet soon turned pirate again, but still bad at it, he was quickly caught and hanged.

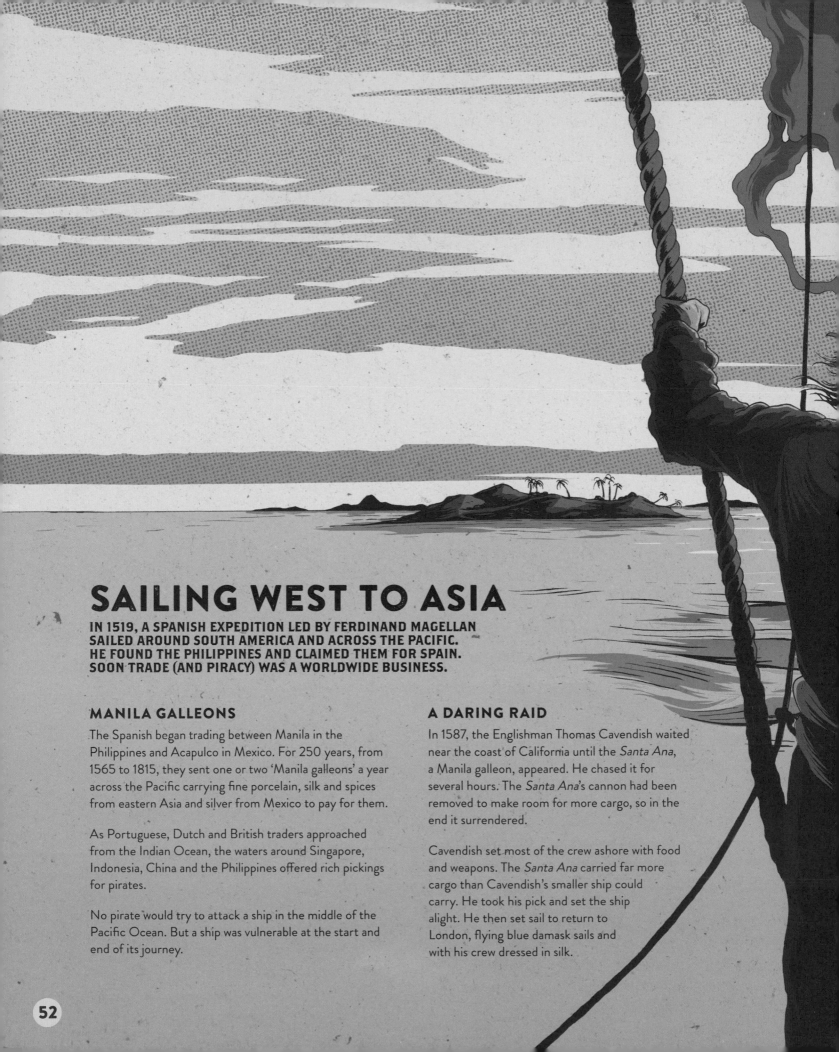

SAILING WEST TO ASIA

IN 1519, A SPANISH EXPEDITION LED BY FERDINAND MAGELLAN SAILED AROUND SOUTH AMERICA AND ACROSS THE PACIFIC. HE FOUND THE PHILIPPINES AND CLAIMED THEM FOR SPAIN. SOON TRADE (AND PIRACY) WAS A WORLDWIDE BUSINESS.

MANILA GALLEONS

The Spanish began trading between Manila in the Philippines and Acapulco in Mexico. For 250 years, from 1565 to 1815, they sent one or two 'Manila galleons' a year across the Pacific carrying fine porcelain, silk and spices from eastern Asia and silver from Mexico to pay for them.

As Portuguese, Dutch and British traders approached from the Indian Ocean, the waters around Singapore, Indonesia, China and the Philippines offered rich pickings for pirates.

No pirate would try to attack a ship in the middle of the Pacific Ocean. But a ship was vulnerable at the start and end of its journey.

A DARING RAID

In 1587, the Englishman Thomas Cavendish waited near the coast of California until the *Santa Ana*, a Manila galleon, appeared. He chased it for several hours. The *Santa Ana*'s cannon had been removed to make room for more cargo, so in the end it surrendered.

Cavendish set most of the crew ashore with food and weapons. The *Santa Ana* carried far more cargo than Cavendish's smaller ship could carry. He took his pick and set the ship alight. He then set sail to return to London, flying blue damask sails and with his crew dressed in silk.

UNDERSEA TREASURE

The Manila galleons faced danger from storms and from being wrecked on shallow coral reefs. Around a hundred were lost, and their treasure probably still lies beneath the sea. Hoards of gold and silver from the Americas, and exotic cargoes of silk, jade, pearls, jewels, spices and porcelain from Asia wait to be found by modern divers.

SHARING THE SPOILS

Chinese, Japanese and Korean pirates dominated the China Sea. They sailed in junks, which were very agile and much faster than the lumbering ships used by European pirates.

Small-time pirates fished in winter and turned to piracy in summer. Groups of up to 20 men in one or two junks would carry out a raid. Once they had taken enough iron tools, food and other objects to keep themselves alive for a few months, they would disband again.

Professional pirates, such as the terrifying wokou, were a different matter entirely...

CHINA SEA

AS NEW TRADING LINKS WERE FORGED WITH THE EAST, THE WATERS OF THE CHINA SEA BECAME RICH PICKINGS FOR SOME OF THE MOST NOTORIOUS AND MERCILESS PIRATES OF THEM ALL.

WINE IS BAD FOR YOU

1556: the general Hu Dongxian stocked a ship with poisoned wine. The crew abandoned the ship when the wokou appeared, leaving the pirates to drink the wine ... and die.

A SAFE PLACE

The islands off the coast of Ningbo became a pirate haven in the 1540s, enjoyed by Portuguese as well as Asian pirates.

CLEARING THE COAST

1661–1663: coastal regions from Fujiang to Zhejiang were evacuated to nearly 20 km inland to stop sea-borne rebels and pirates getting supplies. It was very hard on local people.

ROBBER ISLANDS

The Portuguese called the islands near Guangzhou, including Hong Kong, the Islas Ladrones, which means 'robber islands' because piracy was rife there.

A PIRATE FAMILY

When a Vietnamese fleet sailed to China in 1792 to recruit pirates to attack China, Zheng Yi joined up. His widow would later become the greatest pirate leader in Chinese history.

BEWARE THE BOGEYMAN

Fierce Indonesian Buginese pirates who sailed from Singapore to the Philippines were so feared that the term 'bogeyman' comes from their name.

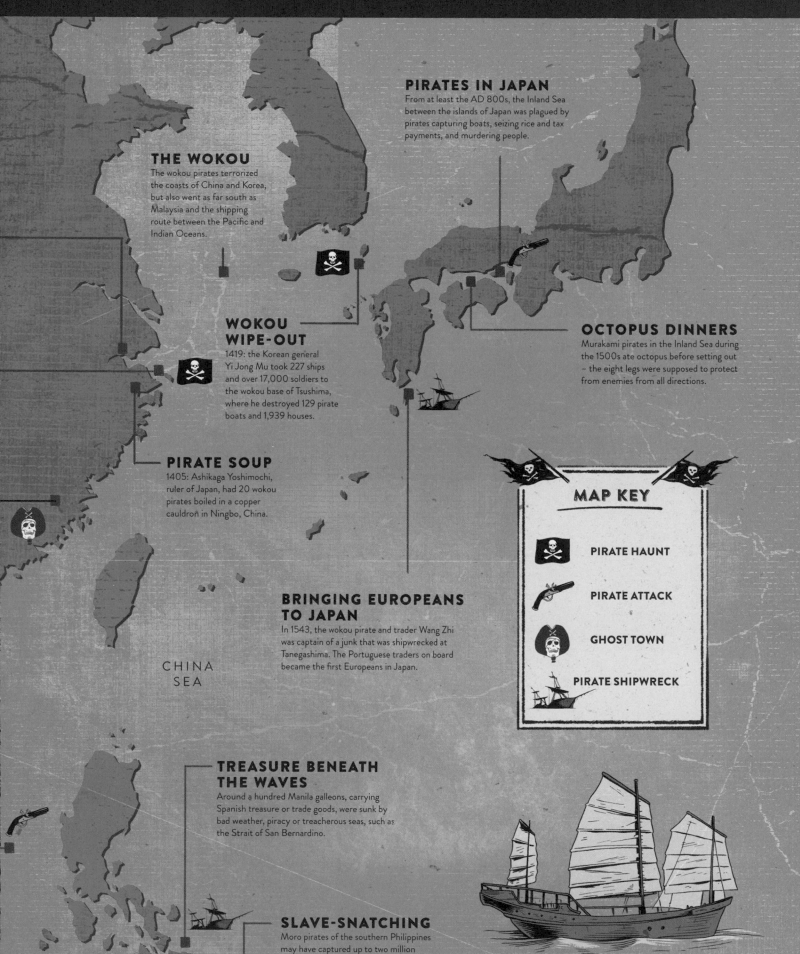

PIRATES IN JAPAN

From at least the AD 800s, the Inland Sea between the islands of Japan was plagued by pirates capturing boats, seizing rice and tax payments, and murdering people.

THE WOKOU

The wokou pirates terrorized the coasts of China and Korea, but also went as far south as Malaysia and the shipping route between the Pacific and Indian Oceans.

WOKOU WIPE-OUT

1419: the Korean general Yi Jong Mu took 227 ships and over 17,000 soldiers to the wokou base of Tsushima, where he destroyed 129 pirate boats and 1,939 houses.

OCTOPUS DINNERS

Murakami pirates in the Inland Sea during the 1500s ate octopus before setting out – the eight legs were supposed to protect from enemies from all directions.

PIRATE SOUP

1405: Ashikaga Yoshimochi, ruler of Japan, had 20 wokou pirates boiled in a copper cauldron in Ningbo, China.

MAP KEY

PIRATE HAUNT

PIRATE ATTACK

GHOST TOWN

PIRATE SHIPWRECK

BRINGING EUROPEANS TO JAPAN

In 1543, the wokou pirate and trader Wang Zhi was captain of a junk that was shipwrecked at Tanegashima. The Portuguese traders on board became the first Europeans in Japan.

CHINA SEA

TREASURE BENEATH THE WAVES

Around a hundred Manila galleons, carrying Spanish treasure or trade goods, were sunk by bad weather, piracy or treacherous seas, such as the Strait of San Bernardino.

SLAVE-SNATCHING

Moro pirates of the southern Philippines may have captured up to two million slaves between 1565 and 1765 from areas ruled by the Spanish.

PIRATES OF EASTERN ASIA

EUROPEAN PIRATES ARRIVING IN THE CHINA SEA WERE OUTNUMBERED BY THE ASIAN PIRATES ALREADY AT WORK AROUND THE MANY ISLANDS OF THE AREA.

THE WICKED WOKOU

From 1350 to 1567, a mix of Japanese, Chinese and Korean pirates called wokou specialized in raids on the coast, terrorizing villages and towns, particularly in China. A ban on trade between China and Japan encouraged piracy and smuggling, as the only ways people could get hold of foreign goods.

Wokou raids crippled parts of China and Korea. The wokou were so certain of success that they sometimes burned their own boats when they landed to raid, making the point that they were not going to retreat. When they wanted to leave, they seized other boats.

THE ZHENG PIRATE FAMILY

Zheng Zhilong was a successful pirate who, by 1627, had his own fleet. The coastal towns and villages of China lived in fear of his raids. Trade all but stopped under the threat of his attacks.

It was common for Chinese pirates to behead their victims and hang the heads around their own necks, looping the victim's long pigtail to form a gruesome necklace.

In 1628, Zheng defeated the official Chinese fleet and agreed to work as a pirate hunter. But he continued to run a fleet of 1,000 pirate ships and soon ruled the coast from Guangzhou to the Yangtze River. He lived in splendour, surrounded by Dutch soldiers as bodyguards and waited on by a troop of 300 ex-slaves dressed in bright silks.

Zheng was executed in 1661. His son, Zheng Chenggong, and his son after him, continued the family business with huge success.

GROWING PIRATE FLEETS

In the 1700s and 1800s, pirate fleets grew even larger. The most successful pirates operated like businesses, keeping full records and accounts. The huge fleets preyed mercilessly on the trade routes around China, particularly along the south coast.

In 1802, Zheng Yi, another member of the famous pirate family, took over a fleet of ships previously ruled by his cousin, Zheng Qi, and was soon leader of the most daunting pirate fleet ever seen.

FLOOD-DRAGONS AND BLACK DEMONS

Those preyed on by the wokou were terrified of them. It was said they could stay underwater for a long time, that they were 'flood-dragons' causing floods and storms, and that they did not sink in water.

Zheng Shi

Beautiful, slender

Strict & Ruthless

58

THE MOST SUCCESSFUL PIRATE OF ALL TIME WAS ZHENG SHI, OR 'WIDOW OF ZHENG'. SHE TERRORIZED THE SEA AROUND CHINA IN THE EARLY 1800S, COMMANDING MORE THAN 70,000 PIRATES.

BORN: c.1775. **ACTIVE:** 1801–1810, China Sea. **DISTINGUISHING FEATURES:** Beautiful, slender; strict and ruthless. **WANTED FOR:** Raids on riverside and coastal villages, and shipping in the China Sea.

MARRIAGE TO A PIRATE

Zheng Shi was born Shi Xianggu in Guangdong province. She worked as an entertainer of sailors in bars until she was spotted – or possibly captured – by the successful pirate Zheng Yi in 1801. She agreed to marry him only as long as she had an equal part in his business.

Together, they built his fleet from 200 to around 1,800 ships. It was a confederation of pirates, who found strength working together. The confederation was divided by colour, with black, white, blue, yellow and green fleets led by the Red Flag Fleet.

GOING IT ALONE

Only six years after their marriage, Zheng Yi died. Zheng Shi could have lived quietly as a wealthy widow, but decided instead to run the fleet herself.

RUNNING A TIGHT SHIP

Zheng Shi drew up a strict code of conduct and a business-like system for dealing with plunder. One fifth of plundered goods was shared among the successful ship's crew, then the rest was used to buy supplies, and pay crews, spies and other workers. Zheng Shi concentrated on the business aspects of the fleet, leaving control of the ships, sailing and fighting to her second-in-command, Zhang Baozai.

The fleet attacked Chinese shipping, and the British and Portuguese ships that came to trade with China. The shallow-bottomed junks even sailed inland up rivers and terrorized villages and towns, seizing goods or demanding protection money.

BEAUTIFUL BUT BRUTAL

Zheng Shi inflicted savage punishments on pirates who broke her code. For disobedience, stealing from the plunder, and most other crimes, a pirate was beheaded and his body thrown into the sea. Deserters, if caught, had an ear cut off. Zheng Shi was concerned about the treatment of women. A pirate was allowed to marry a captured woman but then must be faithful to her. Anyone who mistreated a woman was executed.

PEACEFUL RETIREMENT

Zheng Shi's fleet was larger than the official navy of most countries, and all sailors feared it. The Chinese navy failed again and again to defeat her, even with the help of English and Portuguese bounty-hunters. Instead, she captured many of the ships and crew sent against her, adding them to her fleet.

Eventually, Zheng Shi had had enough. She ended her career on her terms, negotiating with the Emperor's forces so that she and most of her 70,000–80,000 pirates could keep their wealth and go free. Zheng Shi married Zhang Baozai and ran a gambling shop until her peaceful death at the age of 69.

LANDLUBBING

AS A PIRATE, YOU SPEND WEEKS OR EVEN MONTHS AT A TIME AT SEA. WHAT ARE YOU LOOKING FORWARD TO MOST WHEN YOU REACH LAND?

CAREENING YOUR SHIP

Unfortunately, work doesn't stop because you're on land. After months at sea, especially in tropical waters, your ship is dirty, worm-eaten and covered in barnacles.

You need to scrape off the shellfish, treat the wood to keep it waterproof and mend any broken or rotten parts. Your life depends on your ship being sea-worthy and fast enough to get you out of trouble.

FILL YOUR FACE!

Weeks of awful food have made you ravenous. Fresh fruit provides vitamins. Fresh meat and eggs are welcome after a long period of either no meat or chewy, dried, salty meat.

PARTY!

While on board, you drink grog – water, rum and sugar – but drunkenness is forbidden. You need your wits about you. On shore, there are tons of temptations – booze, gambling or catching the eye of good-looking locals. Or maybe you already have a sweetheart waiting for you.

SAILORS CALLED THOSE WHO SPENT THEIR TIME ON LAND 'LANDLUBBERS'.

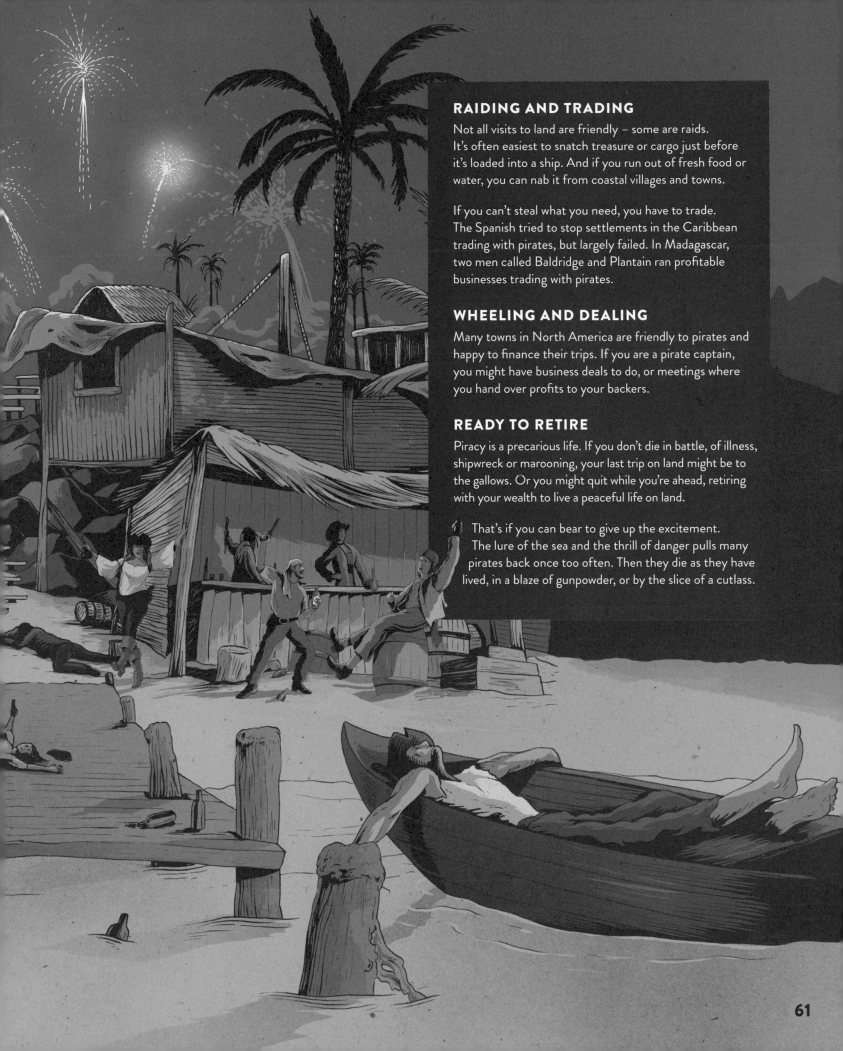

RAIDING AND TRADING

Not all visits to land are friendly – some are raids. It's often easiest to snatch treasure or cargo just before it's loaded into a ship. And if you run out of fresh food or water, you can nab it from coastal villages and towns.

If you can't steal what you need, you have to trade. The Spanish tried to stop settlements in the Caribbean trading with pirates, but largely failed. In Madagascar, two men called Baldridge and Plantain ran profitable businesses trading with pirates.

WHEELING AND DEALING

Many towns in North America are friendly to pirates and happy to finance their trips. If you are a pirate captain, you might have business deals to do, or meetings where you hand over profits to your backers.

READY TO RETIRE

Piracy is a precarious life. If you don't die in battle, of illness, shipwreck or marooning, your last trip on land might be to the gallows. Or you might quit while you're ahead, retiring with your wealth to live a peaceful life on land.

That's if you can bear to give up the excitement. The lure of the sea and the thrill of danger pulls many pirates back once too often. Then they die as they have lived, in a blaze of gunpowder, or by the slice of a cutlass.

GLOSSARY

Barbary coast
The coastal regions of North Africa lived in by the Berber people

boatswain
The crew member in charge of the decks

bowsprit
Spar (like a pole) sticking out at the front of a ship

bribe
Try to make someone do something by giving them money or rewards

buccaneer
A pirate who attacked Spanish ships in the Caribbean in the 17th century

careening
Landing a ship for maintenance; cleaning and repairing it

cholera
An infection of the small intestine caused by bacteria

confederation
An organization formed from a number of different groups into an alliance

conquistadores
Adventurers from Spain and Portugal who invaded and conquered the countries of South America

corsair
A pirate licensed by a state to act as a pirate; also called a privateer

crusader
Someone who took part in the Crusades (see below)

Crusades
Medieval Christian invasions of Middle Eastern countries, aiming to capture Jerusalem from Islamic rule

disembowel
Kill someone by removing the stomach and intestines

draught (of a ship)
The distance between the surface of the sea and the lowest part of the ship

East India Company
A company set up by a nation state to carry out trade with the East Indies, but usually trading also with India and China

flagship
The best and leading ship in a navy or company, which carries the commander of the fleet and can fly a special flag

galley (ship)
A ship propelled by a large number of rowers, often slaves, who sit on benches in the lower part of the ship. Most galleys also had sails

galley (part of a ship)
The kitchen in a ship

governor
An official who is in charge of a particular territory or region

grounded (as in ships)
To become stuck because the bottom of the ship has run into land

guild
A professional group for people who have a particular craft

gunner
The crew member in charge of the cannons

Knights Hospitaller
Medieval soldiers who were originally crusaders but became pirates

letter of marque
Official letter authorizing someone to act as a privateer – a pirate in the service of the state

license
Grant official permission to do or own something

maroon
To leave on an island as a punishment; marooned people were expected to die of starvation or thirst

master
The navigator on a ship, who is in charge of reading maps and reading the stars

Moghul
Belonging to the Moghul Empire, an empire in northern India and modern-day Afghanistan

Ottoman
Belonging to the Ottoman Empire, which ruled Turkey from the 13th to the 20th centuries

pillage
Loot and ransack

pirate
A person who attacks and robs boats and coastal settlements, stealing goods and often killing or kidnapping people

plantation
A large farm where plants are grown for commercial use eg. sugar plantation

privateer
A person licensed by a state to act as an official pirate; also called a corsair

profligate
Extravagant and sometimes immoral

ransom
A sum of money or other reward demanded for the release of a kidnapped person or object

renegade
A person who deserts an organization or country

share (as in buying a share)
A portion of a business

smuggling
Secretly taking things into a country without paying any taxes or other dues

Spanish Main
The mainland coasts around Mexico and the Caribbean that were controlled by Spain in the 16th and 17th centuries

treasure ships / fleet
A group of ships carrying treasure that sailed together for protection

yardarm
Horizontal spars (or beams) from which square sails are hung on a sailing ship

INDEX